CONTENTS

CREDITS

Author and Artist: Joni Prittie

Photographer: Todd Tsukushi

Makeup and Hair: Allison Kelsen, Facial Impressions

Special thanks to our beautiful models

ISBN 0-937769-53-3

IRON-ON TRANSFER INSTRUCTIONS

Wearing hand painted clothing is great fun. Giving presents you make is always enjoyable.

Art-to-wear clothing is easy as one, two, three with this complete iron-on transfer book. All of the basic steps are accompanied by illustrated, step-by-step instructions to help you achieve stunning effects. You can create beautiful clothing and accessories with confidence and perhaps even start your own art-to-wear business!

Before you begin...

- Read all instructions and tips carefully
- Gather materials for project

SUPPLIES

- Iron-on transfer
- Cardboard to fit in shirt
- Sharp scissors
- Squeeze bottle fabric paints
- Iron
- Paper towel or soft cloth
- Ironing board
- Decorative trims (optional)
- Pre-washed sweatshirt or item to be decorated
- Fabric glue if trim is used

To begin...

- Protect your ironing board cover with a clean cloth
- Pre-wash and dry garment to remove sizing, paint will have a better grip on unsized fabrics.
- Preheat iron to recommended temperature for the fabric you are decorating. DO NOT USE STEAM!

DESIGN TRANSFER

Step 1. Cut out the transfer design carefully. Cut off lines or parts of the design you do not want to transfer.

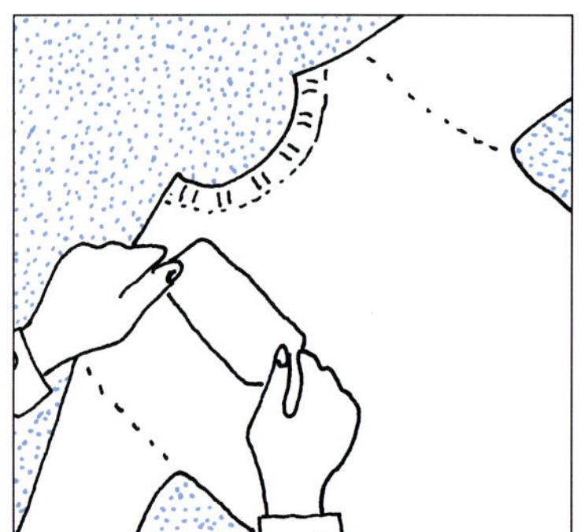

Step 2. Position the selected transfer design in the desired location on the right-side of the fabric—INK-SIDE DOWN.

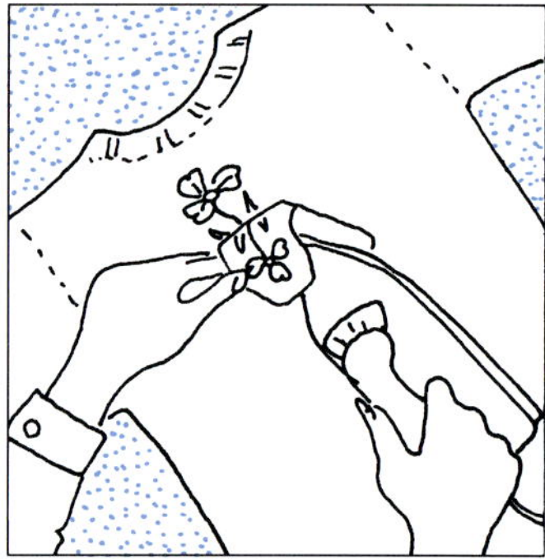

Step 3. Place the preheated iron directly on the transfer pattern. Press, lift an edge of the transfer paper, while holding the rest of the design in place. Look to see if the ink has transferred.

DO NOT SLIDE THE IRON THE WAY YOU DO WHEN IRONING—THE DESIGN COULD SMEAR. Lift the iron directly off the garment and allow the transfer paper to remain in place until cool. Lift the transfer paper off of the garment.

TIP: Transfers can be used more than once, but they get lighter with each use. Use the shortest amount of ironing time possible for a clear transfer and transfer will be reusable! When reusing a transfer design, place a piece of aluminum foil on the ironing board under the fabric; this will allow for a darker transfer of the ink.

TIP: Place a piece of cardboard inside the garment, under the area to be painted. This will prevent paint from bleeding through. Paint along the outlines of the design or fill in the shapes with color. Complete painting instructions are on the following page.

TRANSFERS APPLIED BY FUSING

In addition to basic supplies, you will need...

• White or a light-colored printed cotton— the design will be ironed to this fabric.
• Fusible webbing or fusible sheeting—follow instructions that are included with the webbing or sheets for proper heat setting.

Note: Fusible webbing or sheets can be purchased at your local fabric store.

Do you want to use your iron-on transfer design on denim or dark fabric? Simply, follow these easy steps.

Step 1. Cut out the selected iron-on transfer design.

Step 2. Follow the transfer instructions and iron the design to a light-colored cotton.

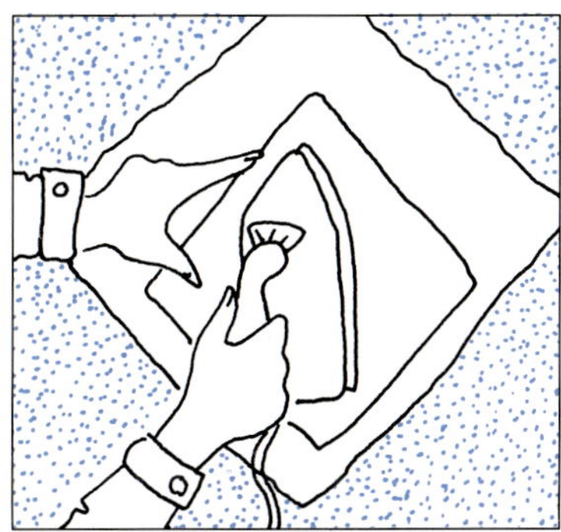

Step 3. Iron fusible sheet to reverse side of fabric. Be sure all of the design is backed by fusible material.

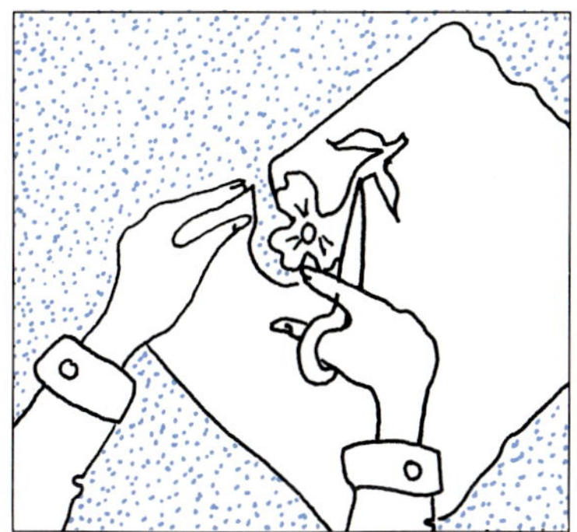

Step 4. Cut out the iron-on transfer design by following the outside edge of the pattern. Peel the paper backing from the fusible material.

Step 5. Place the cut out iron-on transfer on denim or dark clothing and iron the design in place.

Step 6. Paint and decorate the design!

ART-TO-WEAR CARE

Hand washing and hanging to dry are the safest ways to clean hand decorated clothing. If you are machine washing, turn the garment inside out or place in a pillow case (twist tie the pillow case closed) and wash on delicate cycle. Machine drying can crack and dry fabric paints. In addition, ironing the painted area is not recommended.

PAINTING INSTRUCTIONS

Transfer ink is not permanent on 100% cotton. On polyester blends the ink is permanent.

Painting on fabric is easy. Visit your favorite fabric or craft store for the latest in fabric paints. Any type of acrylic paint will work on fabric because it is permanent and holds beautiful color.

Small squeeze bottles of fabric paint are wonderful because there is no need for brushing paint on; simply, squeeze paint from the tube to form lines and fill in the shapes with the bottle tips.

Paints To Try: These are descriptions, not brand names

SLICK PAINT - it has a glossy plastic finish - slick gives a bright shiny "wet" look

SHINY PAINT- it gives a glossy "wet" look with great colors

PEARLIZED - pearlized dry paint creates a glowing pearl effect

IRIDESCENT- iridescent paint has a soft shimmering effect, beautiful for floral designs and evening wear.

GLITTERING - when glittering have glitter mixed in the paint, this is a great way to have a glittery effect without glitter shedding.

GLOW IN THE DARK - paint that stores light and will glow brightly in the dark. Try it for Halloween and childrens' bedtime clothing and accessories.

FLUORESCENT - for day glow brights and neon color effects

Helpful paint supplies

- Brushes - #4 watercolor
- 1/4 inch flat brush
- Permanent fabric marker pen
- Drop cloth for color wash painting
- Paper towel for wiping the brush
- Cup of clean water for brush cleaning

Note: Most samples shown were done with squeeze bottle paints only.

TIP: Work from the top to the bottom, this will save you from touching wet paint!

Storing Paint:
Store paint with caps on securely. Squeeze bottle paints often get air bubbles, so store them upside down to reduce bubbles.

PAINTING INSTRUCTIONS

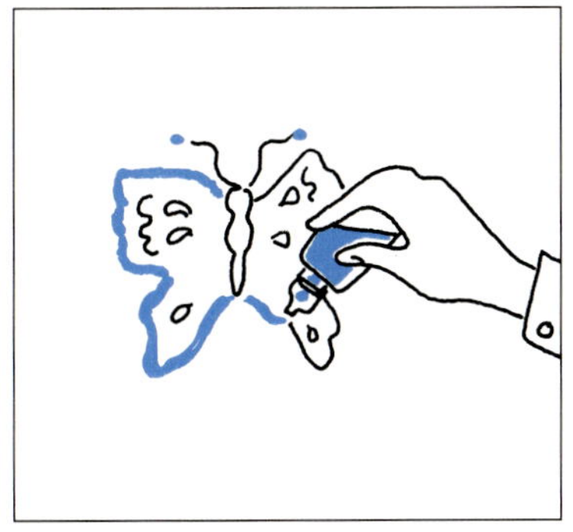

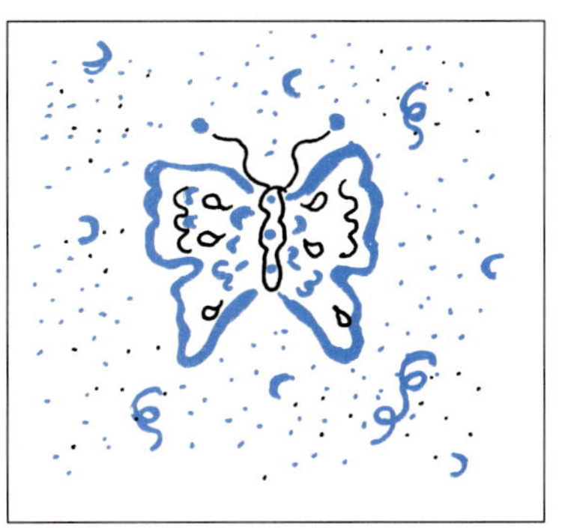

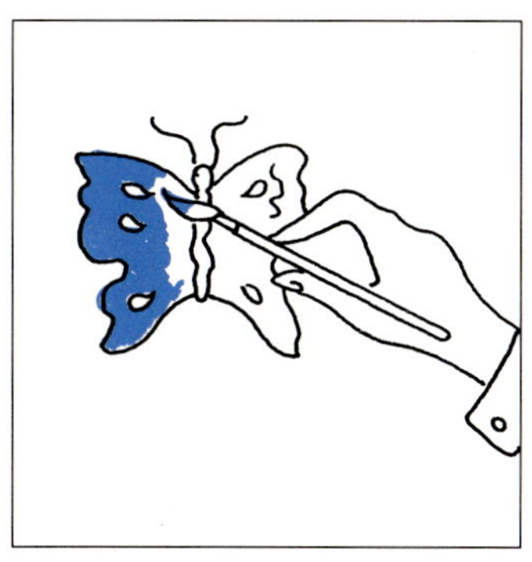

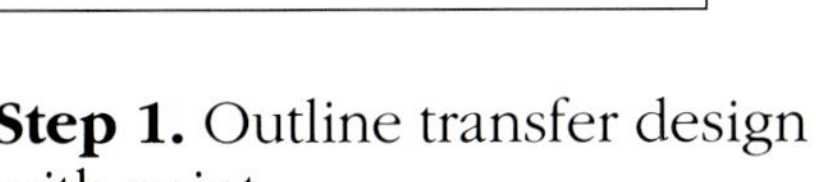

Step 1. Outline transfer design with paint

Step 2. Add freehand squiggles or dots

Step 3. Paint in transfer shape with flat color

TIP: Allow flat color to dry before outlining with a second color

TIP: Sprinkle with glitter while outline is wet, then dry and shake off excess glitter. Or practice on a scrap of fabric to get the effect you want ...

COLOR WASH WITH PAINT

Dilute acrylic paint with water and apply to the design with a wet brush... paint will bleed beyond the lines of the transfer design. Allow the color wash to dry and outline with squeeze bottle paints — add freehand strokes to create a loose look. Allow four hours for the paint to dry completely.

Dry painted clothing flat and do not launder garment for 24 hours.

Freehand:
Freehand strokes will add life to your design. Practice on paper to loosen up and remember that your strokes make the design an original.

Color Washes:
Dilute acrylic or squeeze bottle paints by mixing a 50/50 ratio to water. Brush this on with a wet brush. In order to spread the paint, brush over the area while it is still wet by using clean water. You can also spray an area with clean water before color washing to give paint soft edges.

Splash and Splatter:
Full strength or diluted paint can be splattered on garment with a paint brush. For a finer effect, dip an old toothbrush into the paint, shake off the excess paint carefully and flick the toothbrush with your thumb. This takes a bit of practice but the effect is great!

Circles:
Use a dinner plate for a perfect circle design. Simply, position the plate in the center of the garment and make small dots with your fabric marker pen. Use the dots as a guide when ironing on the transfer.

Mistakes:
There are no mistakes in art but if you have an unplanned drip or dot, try making it into an extra leaf or element of the design. Sometimes adding more dots in that area works well. If the drip or smear is large and cannot be remedied, try using the fusing technique or fabric glue to add a design over the area. A drip can sometimes be removed if sponged at once with warm water.

DECORATING WITH TRIM

Adding trims and notions to art-to-wear will give your shirt or garment added dimension.

Follow trim manufacturer's instructions for attachment.

Craft shops and fabric stores have good selections to choose from.

Heavy duty craft and fabric glue will usually hold rhinestones and flat backed trims through multiple washings.

Trims to try...

MOVABLE EYES for children's clothing

BELLS - sew in place for Christmas and children's trim

POM-POMS sewn or glued in place for bunny tails

PEARLS for day or evening trim—sew or glue in place

LARGE RHINESTONES - glue stone in place and create a permanent setting for a stone by dotting glittery paint all around, as shown.

GLITTER - shake on liberally while paint is still wet. Glitter will not adhere permanently to paint that has been diluted or brushed thinly. Flat colored and metallic glitters will cover paint completely. Opalescent flake glitter will allow the paint color to come through. Experiment with different colors. Place garment over a large box or newspaper while shaking glitter.

PORCELAIN FLOWERS - Add to Victorian and floral designs for a soft-look. Launder the garment inside out.

BUTTONS - Simply, sew in place.

RIBBONS - Tiny bows on little girls shirts are very sweet. Bows are best tied and placed with small safety pins to allow for easy removal during washing.

Embroidery with iron-on transfers...

Transfer design to plain cotton or linen, use a light color so your design transfers well.

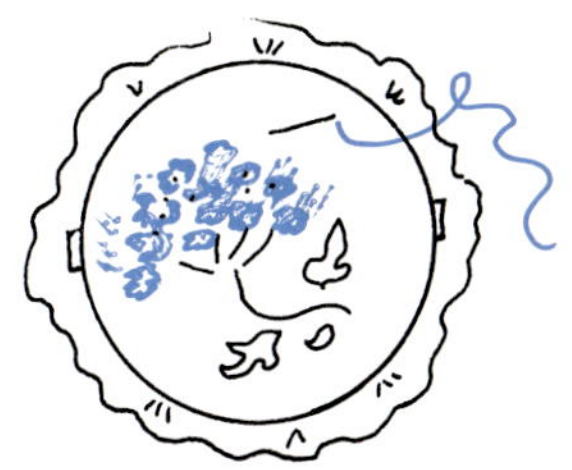

Place fabric in an embroidery hoop and stitch.

Transfer a design to a plain tote bag. Paint and decorate it to coordinate with your painted shirt.

Try painted fabric for pillows.

Frame a painted design for a child's room. Transfer to plain cotton, paint and place in a colorful frame.

Make greeting cards by carefully ironing the transfer to heavy paper. The iron must be used lightly, so the paper does not burn.

Decorating with iron-on transfers...

Place mats, napkins, tablecloths and tea cozies can be decorated with iron-on transfers. If you are working with a quilted item, simply transfer the design to plain cloth and fuse the cloth to the quilting before painting. Fusing instructions are on page two.

Iron-on transfers can also be used on wood. Unpainted, unstained wood will take transfers nicely. Begin with a wood surface that is clean and dust free. Simply, iron design in place, as you would on cloth, make sure you are careful not to scorch wood surfaces that are exposed to the iron. A light cloth placed over the transfer edges will protect the wood. Apply the paint with a brush, using acrylic paints; then lightly varnish the finished piece.

TIP: Dry, painted design and try a very light stain that is applied over the entire piece. This will give the paint an aged look. Always try a pre-test on scrap wood.

* note - remember to cut away all page numbers, notes and Test patterns - before ironing design to garment

cut along line

Test me on your fabric

cut along line

Test me on
your fabric

cut along line
Test me on your fabric

cut along line

cut along line

Test me on your fabric

cut along line

Test me on your fabric

cut along line

Test me on your fabric

Cut along line

Test me on your fabric

cut along line

cut along line

Test me on your fabric

cut along line

Color tip -
American Southwest
Turquoise
Peach
Rust
PINK
Test me on your fabric...
cut along line
test me on your fabric

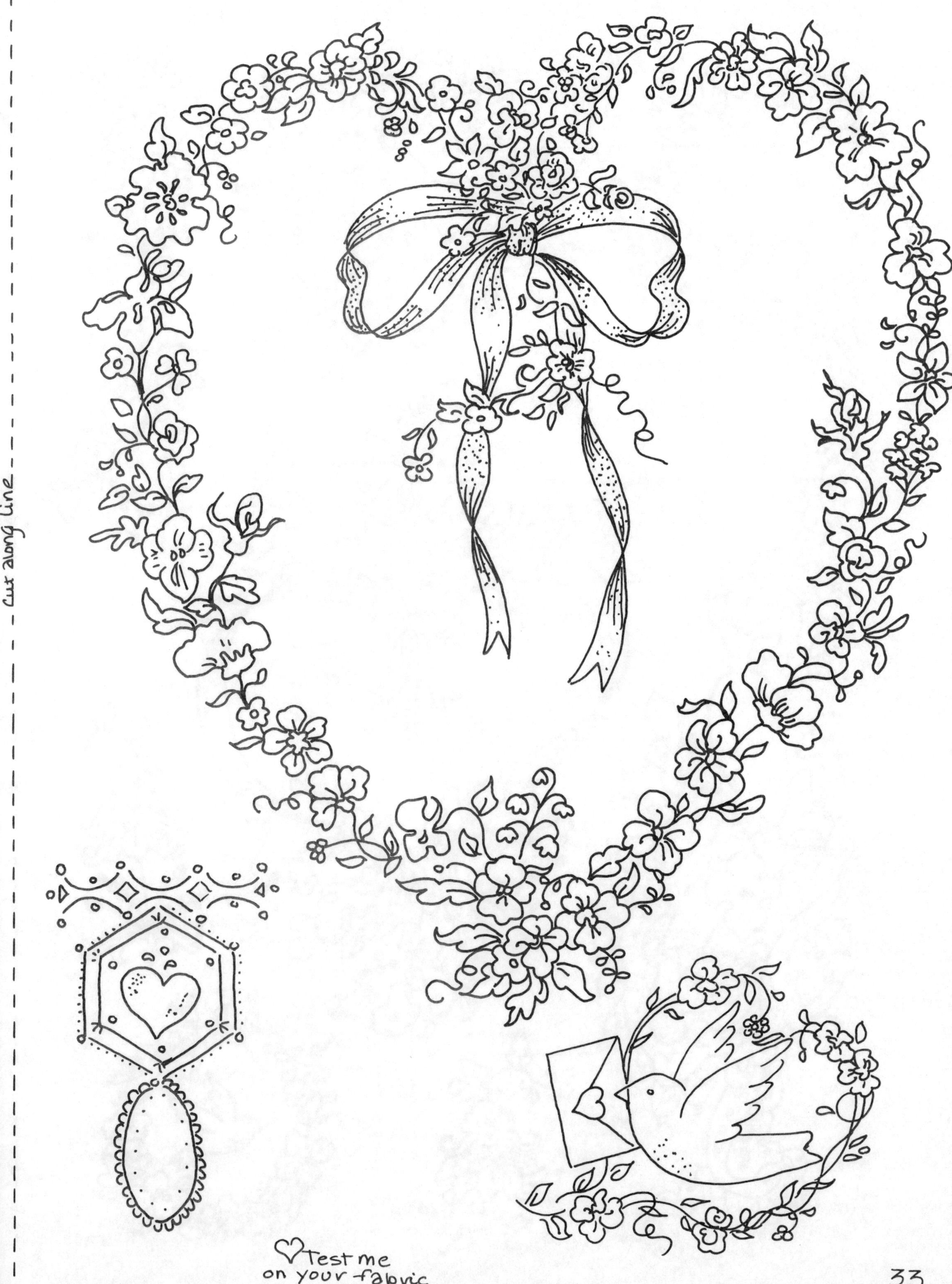
Cut along line
Test me
on your fabric

Cut along Line

cut along line
Iron this design on to white cotton...
follow fusing instructions - fuse to sweatshirt
or blouse at neckline for a Victorian collar.
Design tip...
glue or sew
pearls on
small o!
Test me
on your
fabric

Cut along line
This design was used for cover photo
Test me on your fabric

cut along line

Test me
on your fabric

* note - be sure to cut page numbers away before ironing (also this note!)

cut along line

cut along line

Test me on your fabric

cut along line

cut along line

cut along line

Test me on your fabric

Cut along Line
HONEY

cut along line
Test me
on your fabric

Cut along line

cut along line

HAPPY
BIRTHDAY
cut along line
Test me on
your fabric

Cut along Line

Test me
on your
fabric

Cut along Line

cut along line

Cut along line

Cut along Line

cut along line

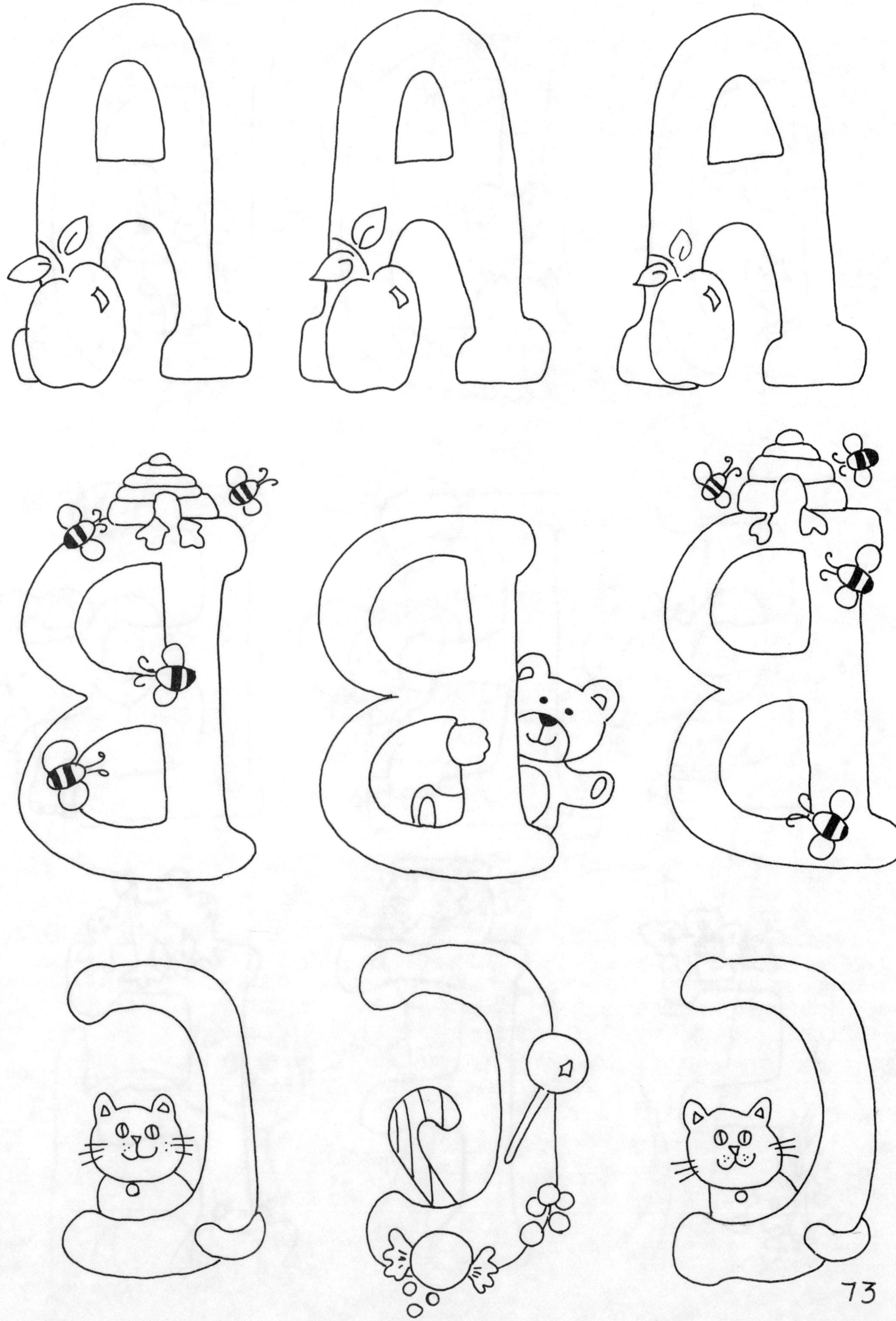

cut along line

cut along line

Cut Along Line

Cut along line

cut along line

Cut along Line

cut along line